CONTENTS

CHURCHILL'S LOST LETTERS   4

BUILD-UP TO CONFLICT   12

HITLER: A PUBLIC'S ENEMY   30

RECRUITMENT   32

ALL FOR ONE & ONE FOR ALL   34

THE GRIM REALITIES OF WAR   48

REMEMBER THE CHILDREN   50

WOMEN AT WAR   56

WAR OVER AIR, LAND AND SEA   62

KEEP SMILING THROUGH   78

CHRISTMAS AT WAR   82

A Mirror publication
Marketing Manager: Fergus McKenna
Mirrorpix: David Scripps and Alex Waters
020 7293 3858

Produced by Trinity Mirror Sport Media,
PO BOX 48, Liverpool L69 3EB
0151 227 2000

Executive Editor: Ken Rogers
Senior Editor: Steve Hanrahan
Senior Art Editor: Rick Cooke
Senior Production Editor: Paul Dove
Compiled and written by: William Hughes
Designer: Glen Hind

Part of the Mirror Collection
© Published by Trinity Mirror
Images: Mirrorpix, PA Photos
Printed by PCP

04

CHURCHILL'S LOST LETTERS

WHILE THE GLOBAL SITUATION BECAME INCREASINGLY TENSE AS SPRING 1939 TURNED
TO SUMMER, WINSTON CHURCHILL WROTE A SERIES OF EXCLUSIVE COLUMNS FOR THE
DAILY MIRROR. APPEARING EVERY FORTNIGHT, THEY SPELT OUT HIS HOPES AND FEARS

CHURCHILL WRITES FOR US NOW

Warns Hitler: "No blood will flow, UNLESS—"

Mr. Winston Churchill, the most trusted statesman in Britain, is to write regularly for the "Daily Mirror." His articles will appear every second Thursday.

TO-DAY WE PRINT HIS FIRST ARTICLE IN THIS IMPORTANT SERIES.

★

THE hush which has spread over Europe in these July days gives an opportunity for surveying the anxious scene both in its shadows and in its lights.

The Nazi attempt to wear down the British and French democracies by what is called " a war of nerves," and by wordy abuse, is doomed to failure.

The people of the British Empire and their French allies have passed through too many alternations of hope and disappointment in recent years to be affected in their resolves by any such manœuvres.

If they look up for a moment from the work of defensive preparation upon which they are engaged, it is not because they expect to see anything which will lead them to take a new view of their duty.

NO ONE KNOWS WHAT IS GOING TO HAPPEN ABROAD, NOR WHEN THE WORST MAY HAPPEN.

ALL WE KNOW IS WHAT WE ARE GOING TO DO IF OCCASION SHOULD ARISE.

There never has been in time of peace such complete unanimity in this old island.

Men and women of every walk in life, all classes, creeds and parties, have prepared themselves mentally and morally for the tremendous changes in the daily life of every household which would accompany a war with Nazidom.

A calm, which excites the admiration of American and other foreign visitors, reigns throughout the land.

The only apprehensions are those of individuals who have not yet found their war work, and of the public at large lest our rulers should falter in some crisis not yet defined.

This sombre, phlegmatic composure is founded upon two solid convictions.

First, that we shall not be called upon to fight by his Majesty's Government unless it is absolutely necessary for our safety and honour.

Secondly, that however painful the ordeal may be, and however long it may last, the Nazi power will not be able to destroy the British Empire and the French Republic.

And that in the end the cause of personal freedom and international good faith will stand upon broader, higher and far stronger foundations throughout all Europe, and, indeed, throughout the world . . .

WHETHER WAR WILL COME RESTS ENTIRELY IN THE HANDS OF HERR HITLER AND HIS CIRCLE OF PARTY LEADERS AND PARTY POLICEMEN.

UNLESS HE GIVES THE ORDER NO CANNON WILL FIRE, NO BLOOD WILL FLOW.

If at any time he chooses to turn his face to the light, ceases to vex and harry his neighbours, lays aside the cruel intolerances of which he has become—perhaps against his own better feelings—the embodiment and expression; even a few months and certainly a few years would open a bright future to the German people in common with the wage-earners and workers of every land.

It is vain to seek " living space " with the sword.

Mere accession of conquered territory will only leave the masses poorer than they were before.

Science, on the other hand, and the confident co-operation of "all the men in all the lands" offer endless " living space " to the peoples of the twentieth century.

There are more people living thirty-storeys high in New York City to-day, and living better, than were living on ground there a hundred years ago.

Eighty thousand Jews are dwelling in a high degree of civilisation in the city of Tel Aviv, which when the last war stopped was only a barren beach.

There is nothing in the material sphere that men cannot do if they work together in peace and freedom.

The barbaric method of forcibly super-imposing one population upon another and of exterminating or subjugating the vanquished is hopelessly inefficient and out of date.

Give science its chance !

Re-create the conditions of confidence and enterprise and goodwill !

Without these wealth and well-being will forever elude the clutching hand.

With them it will soon be found that there is plenty of room and plenty of food for all mankind.

What a glory for Germany, having recovered from her defeat, to lead the way !

Let us hope in this solemn hush Herr Hitler will ponder over these simple but vibrant truths.

To-day there is still time. But one more wrongful step, one further outrage, will close these prospects of our generation in smoke and flame.

Then indeed it will be too late.

I well remember how after the failure of the German Army to take Paris in 1914, informal overtures were made through the United States and other neutral countries by the Kaiser's Government for peace negotiations.

BUT THE PEACEFUL COUNTRIES WHO HAD BEEN INVADED AND ASSAILED WOULD NO LONGER HEAR OF PEACE.

THEY THOUGHT ONLY OF VICTORY, AYE, AND RETRIBUTION !

But this war, should it come—which God forfend—will, because of the weapons of air terror, become incomparably more fierce and more impossible to stop.

Whole vast populations will become inflamed personally against one another to a degree unknown for centuries. It will be a inexpiable war.

Let there be no delusions in the Nazi Party and among its grim chiefs that, for instance, Poland, the Baltic States, the Ukraine, Hungary and Rumania could be over-run, and that the aggressors could then turn round and make peace with the Western Powers.

Napoleon, sword in hand, sought victorious peace in every capital in Europe. He sought it in Berlin, in Vienna, in Madrid, in Rome and finally in Moscow. All he found was St. Helena.

Yet there were years in that struggle when England stood quite alone, all the world against her, even the United States. Very different are the conditions which reveal to-day.

To-day the British Empire would move in alliance or in companionship with three-quarters of the entire population of the globe.

If this mighty mass is united in its a or in its sympathies, not by the st diplomacy, or the doubtful ties of

dynastic marriages, or by the hungry lust for booty and aggression—

but by the consciousness of a common cause and of lofty aims, and by that love of freedom and fair-play which rises in the human heart and urges a ceaseless and all-compelling propaganda of its own.

It is the hope that these and similar considerations will be weighed soberly by the German Dictator and even more carefully by his Italian colleague, that may encourage us still to believe in a peaceful outcome.

NEVERTHELESS, LET NO ONE CLOSE HIS EYES TO UGLY FACTS AND EVIL SIGNS.

Europe is more than half-mobilised at this moment.

In Germany all industry is on a war footing.

At least two million German soldiers are already under arms, humane preparations for early action are being made by a despotic organisation which, whatever its internal malaise and stresses, must be expected to function with terrible precision at the outset.

The unaccountable delay—whoever is to blame for it—in concluding a solid, binding, all-in alliance between Britain, France and Russia, aggravates the danger of a wrong decision by Herr Hitler.

It is lamentable indeed that this broad mainsail of peace and strength, which might carry the ship of human fortunes past the reef, should still be flapping half-hoisted in the wind.

The rejection of President Roosevelt's neutrality proposals in the United States Congress could not have come at a more untimely moment.

And it may well be that this perfectly reasonable controversy, unavoidable under the conditions of free Government by which the English-speaking world must stand or fall, may be a potent factor in bringing about what all American citizens most desire to prevent, and have a very serious interest in preventing.

It is of capital importance that Herr Hitler should not be misled into believing that the recent vote on President Roosevelt's Neutrality Bill represents the last word which the United States has to speak upon the fundamental issues now at stake.

"THIS UNACCOUNTABLE DELAY . ." Another month has gone by since Mr. Strang left for Moscow.

THE WATCHDOG OF BRITAIN'S SAFETY . . .

For years he warned us of dangers which have now become terrible realities. For years he pressed for the policy of STRENGTH, which the whole nation now supports.

The cartoon by Low is reproduced by permission of the " Evening Standard." The two little caricatures are reproduced by permission of the proprietors of " Punch."

Opposite: A thoughtful Winston Churchill. He would become a key figure in the War Cabinet formed following the outbreak of hostilities

Above: The first of Churchill's exclusive articles, published in the Mirror on July 13, 1939

05

Thursday, July 27, 1939   THE DAILY MIRROR   Page 15

HITLER SELLS THE PASS!

THE hush continues throughout Europe, and this cheerless summer is enlivened by occasional jets of artificial sunlight from Berlin and Rome.

WE ARE INVITED TO DRAW WHAT COMFORT WE MAY FROM AN OFFICIAL GERMAN DECLARATION THAT THERE MUST BE NO WAR FOR DANZIG.

GERMANY MUST HAVE IT WITHOUT A WAR !

All the time the German Army is steadily being placed upon a war footing. A million reservists have been called up, in addition to the normal army of a million men.

Such a marshalling of strength in time of peace has never before been seen.

It far exceeds the German force gathered for the pretended " manœuvres " of last September.

However, we are assured from Berlin that these preparations are purely defensive. Their only object is to protect innocent, peace-loving Nazidom from some deadly attack by Poland or Denmark or Holland or perhaps from the Grand Duchy of Luxemburg.

Nazi blandishments have not yet attained the success in Britain and France which greeted similar grimaces last year.

It is no mere case of once bit, twice shy. It is a case of thrice bit, once shy.

✦ ✦ ✦

We must be glad that Ministers and some of their experts now assure us of their confidence that our armed forces and preparations are adequate to our dangers.

The Ministers themselves must also be glad to be able to say this; because having had unlimited power all these years, they are undoubtedly responsible, and will be held responsible, for any deficiencies.

A FAR MORE SIGNIFICANT SIGNAL IS MADE TO US FROM THE TYROL.

The more the agreement between the German and Italian Dictators about the future of the Tyrol becomes known, the more we realise how tense and grave is the state of Europe.

It looks as if Herr Hitler has consented to the transfer

Mr. Winston Churchill writes to-day another vital article in his special series for the "Daily Mirror."

Hitler, he says, has taken a step which is "the sacrifice of his very heart's blood."

of the entire German-speaking population of the Province of Bozen either to Greater Germany or elsewhere in Italy, in order that the homelands on which they have dwelt for a thousand years, the valleys and mountains of that beautiful upland, may be populated with Italians.

IN TAKING THIS STEP HE IS SACRIFICING HIS VERY HEART'S BLOOD.

THE UPROOTING OF A GERMANIC PEASANTRY FROM ITS NATIVE SOIL IS A COMPLETE DENIAL OF THE MAIN DECLARED PURPOSE OF HIS LIFE.

It runs counter to the most intense passion, apart from Jew-baiting, which has inspired it.

That he should be willing to do this is a proof, which should be plain to the simplest mind, how seriously he regards the situation, and how determined he is to go forward upon the path of Continental domination.

This was the price —the only price that would serve to bind Mussolini to his chariot wheels.

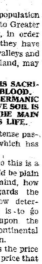

The position of the Italian Dictator has become increasingly precarious.

The association of Italy with Germany has undermined the foundations of Italian national power, and has already deeply affected Italian independence.

Year after year the Italian people have seen tremendous changes to their detriment in the north.

The loss of their influence in Austria, which a few years ago was paramount—

The arrival of powerful German forces at the Brenner Pass—

The naked exposure of German ambitions towards Trieste and the Adriatic—

The arrival in Italy in all kinds of key positions of large numbers of German agents—

The ever-growing ascendancy in the Axis of the senior partner—

ALL HAVE BEEN VIEWED BY THE ITALIAN PEOPLE, AND EVEN IN THE HIGHER CIRCLES OF THE FASCIST PARTY, WITH INCREASING DISMAY.

The prospect of being dragged into a war of the most terrible character with France and Great Britain, in which the first brunt would fall upon Italy, is a cause of fear and anger throughout the whole of the long and vulnerable peninsula.

To wage a war for mortal stakes against the other two great Mediterranean Powers is indeed a tragic task to set a hard-working and hard-pressed population.

The two Western democracies were the chief architects of Italian liberation and Italian unity.

✦ ✦ ✦

To-day, as in the nineteenth century, French and British interests would best be served by a free and prosperous Italy in peaceful partnership of the Mediterranean.

THE SHADE OF GARIBALDI RAISES A WARNING HAND FROM THE PAST.

THE VATICAN HAS MANIFESTED ITS DISAPPROVAL.

NOTHING IS FURTHER FROM THE WISH OF THE ITALIAN PEOPLE THAN TO BE PLUNGED INTO A PERFECTLY NEEDLESS STRUGGLE FOR LIFE WITH THE FRENCH ARMY AND THE BRITISH NAVY.

In such a conflict they could only hope to be upheld by German troops under whose commanders their own army would be forced to serve.

Hundreds of thousands of German soldiers must enter Italy, and be billeted in Italian households.

A total blockade would descend upon their coasts.

Their armies in Libya and Abyssinia are but hostages to sea-power.

In the air race Italy has fallen hopelessly behind, and here again she must look to the air power of Germany as her chief protection.

✦ ✦ ✦

NOT A PLEASANT PROSPECT.

NOT AN EASY WAR. NOT A WAR IN TRUE ITALIAN INTEREST.

A WAR IN WHICH DEFEAT SPELLS RUIN, AND VICTORY PERMANENT SUBORDINATION.

Yet this is the war into which Signor

Mussolini—in whom even those who dislike his system have thought to see a great Italian and a great patriot—is urging the nation he has led so long and from whom he has received so much !

No wonder he must have something to show in compensation for the injuries which Italy has sustained, and the perils upon which he now seeks to launch her.

And Hitler has paid the price.

The sharp talons of Nazidom will pluck up the German-speaking peasants and mountaineers from their homes in the land of Andreas Hofer, and plant them peaceably if they will, forcibly if they won't, upon Italian or German plains.

✦ ✦ ✦

The migration or exchange of populations is not in itself a process necessarily to be excluded from efforts to procure European tranquillity.

Where hostile races are hopelessly and equally intermingled, where no boundary can be delimited, a sorting-out movement may produce good results.

Certainly the exchange of several millions of Turks and Greeks was skilfully accomplished in Thrace and Asia Minor, and has had the best results in the after-relations of the two countries.

But the population of the Tyrol is preponderantly German-speaking.

And the object in this case is not a peaceful settlement of Europe, but a military and strategic step designed to further the waging of a great war by the two Axis Powers.

✦ ✦ ✦

Alarm is caused to Switzerland by the situation in the Tyrol.

The Swiss ask why all tourists have been turned out of the Tyrol at forty-eight hours' notice, and why all foreign residents are to leave the country as soon as possible.

It was suggested as an explanation that

(Continued on Page 19)

by WINSTON CHURCHILL

On the brink: Prime Minister Neville Chamberlain on his way to see the King on the eve of the war

A nation united: Crowds gather to wave to ministers as they arrive at the Houses of Parliament to discuss Hitler's reply to the British Note which led to the declaration of war on Germany on September 3

WINSTON CHURCHILL WRITES—

A WORD TO JAPAN!

Here is another article in the fortnightly series which Mr. Winston Churchill is writing for the "Daily Mirror."

★

MR. CHAMBERLAIN'S reminder to the Japanese Government that Great Britain possesses a superior fleet at home, which might in certain circumstances be sent to the Far East, calls attention pointedly to the mobility of sea-power.

The Japanese know quite well that in the present European situation the British Navy has prior obligations, and that for the time being its mobility is limited to European waters.

But should conditions in Europe change, either by a peaceful solution or a victory of the Peace Block, it would instantaneously revive.

AND ALL OVERSEAS ENTERPRISES UPON WHICH THE JAPANESE ARMY MIGHT BE ENGAGED WOULD, EVEN BEFORE A SHIP WAS MOVED FROM THE ATLANTIC OR MEDITERRANEAN, BECOME SERIOUSLY COMPROMISED.

The TEST is here

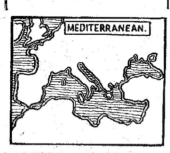

The MEDITERRANEAN: "If Italy's Fleet were beaten in the Mediterranean a day would come when we might expect to obtain more politeness from Japan . . ."

. . . not here

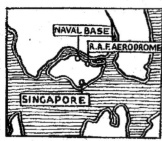

SINGAPORE: "It seems reasonable to suppose that a siege of Singapore will not be undertaken by any Japanese Government not entirely blinded by war fury . . ."

This should be borne in mind when people talk airily of the possibilities of a Japanese attack upon Singapore.

Singapore is as far from Japan as Southampton from New York.

Strong reinforcements of troops have been sent from India to bring its garrison up to full war requirements.

A GREAT FORTRESS LIKE SINGAPORE, ARMED WITH THE HEAVIEST CANNON, AND DEFENDED BY AIRCRAFT AND SUBMARINES, IS IN NO DANGER FROM A PURELY NAVAL ATTACK.

In order to capture Singapore the Japanese would have to send not only their main fleet, but an immense convoy of transports with an army of not less than fifty or sixty thousand men.

These would have to disembark on the peninsula, and begin a regular siege amid its deadly marshes.

♦ ♦ ♦

It would be an operation like the Siege of Port Arthur in 1904, with the difference that all the ceaseless flow of drafts to replace the casualties and wastage of the besiegers would have to be transported across two thousand miles of submarine-infested waters instead of across a few hundred miles before submarines were in effective use.

A stubborn defence should enable the Fortress to hold out for at least nine months or perhaps a year.

If at any moment during this costly and hazardous attack the naval situation in Europe decides itself in favour of Great Britain, a superior British fleet could in a very few weeks enter the Indian Ocean.

This fleet would find on arrival at the Fortress all the docks and workshops which enable the largest battleships to be maintained and repaired.

It could, therefore, enter into the fullest activity from the moment of its arrival.

IT COULD IF NECESSARY FIGHT A MAJOR BATTLE CLOSE TO ITS OWN FIRST-CLASS BASE, WHEREAS THE JAPANESE NAVY WOULD BE TWO THOUSAND MILES FROM A FRIENDLY DOCK.

Simultaneously the communications of the besieging army would be cut, all its sacrifices would be rendered vain, and no prospect but surrender would await its survivors.

It seems, therefore, reasonable to suppose that a siege of Singapore will not be undertaken by any Japanese Government not entirely blinded by war-fury.

♦ ♦ ♦

But the same arguments affect to a large extent the fortunes of the Japanese armies which have invaded China.

The position of these armies is already far from favourable.

They are sprawled over a great part of China.

"We should not hesitate to show the Aggressors that our ships and soldiers will not give way to bullying—BUT WILL FIRE BACK PROMPTLY IF FIRED UPON!"

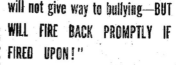

They hold the railroads, several of the greatest cities, and a number of strong posts on the rivers. Around them the whole country is aflame.

The central Chinese Government, under the leadership of their great national leader and commander, Chiang Kai-shek, rules not only in the regions not yet penetrated by the invaders, but over nine-tenths of the territory at this present moment nominally occupied by the Japanese troops.

The Chinese claim that out of 800 counties, to use an English term, their magistrates are carrying on local government uninterruptedly in all but fifty.

♦ ♦ ♦

The guerrillas, backed by the patriotism of a China, united as it has never been united before, wage unceasing warfare, avenged by ferocious reprisals, against the Japanese communications and garrisons.

AND IN THE NORTH—
IS RUSSIA'S ARMY!

The morale of the Japanese nation already shows signs of exhaustion, while the spirit of the Chinese rises with every new atrocity and outrage.

High military opinion in France and England inclines to the view that in another two years China will have defeated Japan.

All the time in the north the formidable Russian Siberian Army and Air Force holds the best army of Japan closely pinned to the frontier, and at any moment a Russian southward movement may compel the

transference of Japanese troops from the south.

If to such a situation there were added at any time a British or American, or best of all a British *and* American, threat to the Japanese communications with China, a catastrophe, unexampled in the history of the Far East, might well overtake the Aggressor.

♦ ♦ ♦

What then are the chances of an improvement in the British naval position in Europe?

The German Navy is not and will not be for the next year or two able to fight a battle outside the Baltic.

IT IS IN THE MEDITERRANEAN THEREFORE THAT THE ANSWER MUST BE SOUGHT.

The British and French Navies should be able to bring at least double the strength in warships against the Italian fleet.

Those who had the opportunity of working with the Italian Navy in the Great War, find it difficult to believe that, ship for ship, and man for man, the Italians are so much superior in quality that they will be able to overcome by personal prowess this immense preponderance of Anglo-French strength.

♦ ♦ ♦

Yet the Italian commitments of large armies in Libya and Abyssinia will require from Signor Mussolini an early fight for the command of the Mediterranean.

If he should lose that fight, as some good judges think he easily might, not only would his African armies be doomed, but far away at the other end of the world the marauding expeditions of Japan would be in deadly peril.

It is to be hoped that these sober considerations will not be lost upon the secret military and naval societies who have taken possession of the Government of Japan.

It may be very pleasant to insult and

(Continued on P. 19)

1939 Timeline

January
In a speech to the Reichstag, Adolf Hitler says: "If the international Jewish financiers in and outside Europe should succeed in plunging the nations once more into a world war, then the result will not be the Bolshevising of the earth and thus the victory of Jewry, but the annihilation of the Jewish race in Europe."

February
The German battleship Bismarck is launched, while Nazis force Jews to hand over all gold and silver items.

March
Hitler declares: "Czechoslovakia has ceased to exist" as German troops occupy the rest of Czechoslovakia - a clear violation of the Munich Agreement of 1938. The German leader also re-iterates his demands against Poland for the return of Danzig and the 'Polish Corridor' to the Reich.

Prime Minister Chamberlain announces British support of Polish independence in an address to the House of Commons.

April
Britain and Poland sign a mutual-assistance pact. USA president Roosevelt seeks assurances from Germany and Italy that they would not attack another European country. However, such assurances were not forthcoming. Hitler and Mussolini knew that Roosevelt was bound by the 1935-1937 Neutrality Acts, preventing America helping either side in the event of war.

Hitler addresses the Reichstag in Berlin. He denounces the 1934 10-year non-aggression pact with Poland and the Anglo-German Naval Agreement of June 1935. Hitler calls the Anglo-Polish Agreement an alliance directed exclusively against Germany and demands the return of Danzig to Germany. Meanwhile, Jews lose tenancy rights and are relocated into Jewish houses.

May
Two warships escort King George VI and Queen Elizabeth to Canada. Each ship carries about 15 million pounds sterling in gold for safekeeping. Turkey and Great Britain conclude a security pact.

June
German Jews are denied the right to hold government jobs, while Winston Churchill urges the British government to form a military alliance with the Soviet Union.

July
Neville Chamberlain's Cabinet met to decide what their course of action would be should the Germans seize Danzig.

German Jews were denied the right to hold government jobs. Meanwhile, Poland presented Britain and France with a German Enigma machine each, having cracked their codes.

August
Albert Forster, Gauleiter for Danzig and Nazi leader, addresses a crowd of 100,000 and says: "The hour of liberation is at hand... our Motherland and our Führer, Adolf Hitler, are determined to support us." A trial blackout is ordered for London in preparation for war.

Hitler reads a telegram from Josef Stalin, acknowledging agreement on a non-aggression pact and responds by banging his fist on a table, shouting: "I have them! I have them!"

Hitler then authorises the killing "without pity or mercy, all men, women and children of Polish descent or language." He also sets a date of September 1 for the invasion of Poland.

Britain and France try to persuade Poland to negotiate with Germany, but she refuses. The British Admiralty assumes control of all British-registered merchant ships as the Royal Navy is put on full alert. Army and navy mobilization is commenced.

Hitler's Directive Number 1 declares that at 4.45am on September 1, German Armed Forces will invade Poland.

September
General mobilisation is declared in Britain on September 1 and, the following day, a national Service Act is passed.

After Germany rejects the Anglo-French ultimatum of September 1 calling for the withdrawal of all German forces from Poland, Britain declares war on Germany at 11am.

October
Men aged between 20 and 22 become liable for conscription in Britain.

November
Queen Elizabeth broadcasts a message to the women of the Empire, calling them to join the war effort. Prime Minister Chamberlain imposes an embargo on all German trade.

December
Ahead of the first Christmas at war, Canadian troops arrive in Britain.

THE DAILY MIR...

Churchill's Opinion!

WINSTON CHURCHILL retur...

Here he sums up the World Crisis

ELEVENTH

IN view of the Soviet-German intrigue and all other information to hand it is becoming increasingly difficult to see how war can be averted. It is certainly not right to give up hope.

BUT EVENTS ARE MOVING FORWARD FROM EVERY QUARTER AND ALONG ALL ROADS TOWARDS CATASTROPHE.

THE GERMAN MILITARY PREPARATIONS HAVE ALREADY REACHED A POINT WHEN ACTION ON THE GREATEST SCALE IS POSSIBLE AT ANY MOMENT.

1914 mobilisation was a lengthy process.

A period of nearly three weeks was required before any main collision was possible

★

But the Germans have now so many divisions on a war-footing opposite the Polish frontiers that they could attack with very large forces within a few hours of the order being given.

It seems probable, therefore, that the warning phase of formal mobilisation will only synchronise with the opening battles in the East.

The French arrangements are also very different from those of 1914.

Then it was thought right to withdraw all French troops ten kilometres from the frontier in order to avoid any appearance of provocation.

But now both nations face each other with large forces and fortifications at close quarters wherever the ground is suitable.

Along the Rhine Frontier the conditions are grim.

The great river flows swiftly by between two unbroken rows of concrete casemates, armed with cannon and separated from the other side by less than three or four hundred yards.

The most extreme vigilance prevails; and in a few minutes the whole of both fronts could come into action.

MOST OF THE BRIDGES FLOAT ON PONTOONS. THESE HAVE ALREADY BEEN DISCONNECTED.

THE OTHERS CAN BE CLOSED OR DESTROYED ALMOST INSTANTANEOUSLY.

At each end of the bridge between Strasbourg and Kehl the middle of the road is blocked by German and French pill-boxes from which cannon, constantly manned, point at one another.

Communication and traffic across the Rhine has practically ceased.

A few trains, carefully examined at each end, pass daily.

A few tourist cars, whose passports are duly visa-ed, cross from time to time.

Otherwise there is a gulf, utter and mournful, between these two great nations of Western Europe.

Standing by the river's brink one sees the Germans finishing their barbed-wire entanglements, and feels one is looking at men who at any moment may become foes, and at cannon which may open fire with the first light of any morning.

★

These conditions reproduce and bring home to us the tragic, doom-laden state of Europe and of the world.

Along all frontiers for many hundreds of miles, hundreds of thousands of men, armed with the most deadly weapons ever known, and behind them many millions more, await a dread signal, which they would instantly obey.

Whence will this signal come?

Poised on top of water towers, these firemen are waging a battle against flames that swept four storeys of a building in London's Farringdon-road yesterday.

Six people who were trapped on the first floor escaped by ladder before the brigade arrived. Four others left the blazing building by climbing out on to the roof and walking across to another block of offices.

As you see from this picture, thousands of people watched the firemen tackle the flames and conquer them after about half an hour. Traffic was held up for three-quarters of an hour.

Due here next Monday is Maureen O'Sullivan, to make with Robert Montgomery at the Denham Studios "A Busman's Honeymoon" for Metro-Goldwyn-Mayer.

And we ask you, ladies, to note the charming ensemble of Maureen as she left Hollywood—the perfect matching and simplicity—A FEATHER IN HER CAP, so to speak!

Don't get your ears wet! Little Londoners who went with the League of Coloured Children's outing to Littlehampton (Sussex) yesterday.

The Little Princess

She's six weeks old Tetarasak — "Power" and "Dignity" in English — daughter of Prince and Princess Chirasakti of Siam, who are seen with her in this picture.

ned from France Last Night

AT THE HOUR!

"If there is friendly action we shall match it on our side. If there is aggression we shall make war . . ."

And these are the men who will lead our armies—General Gamelin of France and Viscount Gort of Britain.

Mr. Winston Churchill, who now writes regularly for the "Daily Mirror," tells you to-day that France is ready !

GAMELIN

GORT

There is only one man who can give it.

THERE HE SITS IN HIS MOUNTAIN VILLA, TORN BY PASSIONS AND FOREBODINGS, BY APPETITES AND FEARS, WITH HIS FINGER MOVING TOWARDS THE BUTTON WHICH, IF HE PRESSES IT, WILL EXPLODE WHAT IS LEFT OF CIVILISATION.

Never before has mortal man wielded the power to bring sorrow and suffering to such vast numbers of the human race.

★

And—whatever happens—never should a single man have such power again.

The safety and the whole future of mankind require that limits should be set to such personal concentrations of the forces of destruction.

But the choice is still open.

There is no truth and no sense in the plea that Hitler has gone too far to stop. He could stop now.

By a single impulse of will-power he could regain the solid foundations of health and sanity.

He has but to send his reservists to their homes, and his example would be followed step by step in every country.

He has but to restore to the Czech nation he freedom, the independence, and the frontiers he solemnly promised at Munich, o bring about an immediate revulsion of eeling in his favour throughout the world.

★

ndeed, a new atmosphere would be ated, in which every problem could be roached calmly and with a sincere 'e to do the best for all.

en indeed the sun would shine. and 'uld find their place in its vitalising

'ndeed the wage-earning masses in

every country could turn the agencies of science, now bent upon their slaughter, to the building of a material and moral well-being, never before in human reach.

The nations which form the anti-aggression front cannot themselves do anything more.

THERE CAN BE NO QUESTION OF BUYING PEACE.

NO FURTHER CONCESSIONS CAN BE MADE TO THREATS OF VIOLENCE.

We cannot pay Germany to leave off doing wrong.

For four long years Nazidom has been breaking Treaties, spending a thousand million sterling a year on armaments, terrorising its neighbours, or actually annexing their territory.

★

It is a comfort in this grave hour that everyone is united.

There is no need for argument.

All classes and all parties in Great Britain and France have made up their minds that they must face whatever is coming to them, and do their best, as they did before.

They cannot forget that every concession made, in a sincere desire to preserve peace, was interpreted in Germany as a proof of weakness and degeneracy.

Every delay in re-armament was attributed to a selfish reluctance to fight.

Every reference to the horrors of war was attributed to unmanly fear.

France and Britain were portrayed as decadent and dying empires, whose possessions would soon be the spoil of the virile and ruthless totalitarian States.

And this came to us from a Germany which, having invaded the lands of its

neighbours, begged for an armistice in the open field without even trying to defend its own frontiers

It came to us from an Italy which, though it chose its own moment for entering the conflict, could not have maintained itself for six months without British coal and steel, and which would have been cut to rags by Germany and Austria but for the powerful aid of French and British bayonets.

The time has come when Nazi words have ceased to count.

It makes no difference whether they are smooth or violent.

Actions alone affect our judgment.

If there is no action against us we shall remain prepared.

IF THERE IS FRIENDLY ACTION WE SHALL MATCH IT ON OUR SIDE.

IF THERE IS RENEWED AGGRESSION, WE SHALL MAKE WAR.

Many people wonder whether such a war would be short or long.

That depends entirely upon whether Nazidom collapses after its first furious plungings or not.

★

Some Nazi leaders seem to indulge the hope that if they gained initial successes against Poland they could then turn round and offer peace to the Western Democracies.

Let them clear their minds of such delusions.

Those who choose the moment for the beginning of wars must not be allowed to choose the date of their ending.

★

If the Nazi regime forces a war upon the world the very existence of free government among men would be at stake.

SUCH A STRUGGLE COULD NOT END UNTIL THE REIGN OF LAW AND THE SOVEREIGN POWER OF DEMOCRATIC AND PARLIAMENTARY GOVERNMENT HAD ONCE AGAIN BEEN ESTABLISHED UPON THOSE MASSIVE FOUNDATIONS FROM WHICH IN OUR CARELESSNESS WE HAVE ALLOWED THEM TO SLIP.

It could not end while any State, even the smallest or weakest, which had been faithful to the Covenant of the League, suffered ill-usage in its rights or territory as a result of brutal violence.

✦ ✦ ✦

BUILD-UP TO CONFLICT

AS HITLER REFUSED TO ENTER INTO NEGOTIATIONS WITH POLAND TO FIND A PEACEFUL
SOLUTION TO THE CRISIS, BRITAIN STOOD FIRM AGAINST THE GERMAN CHANCELLOR.
THESE PAGES CHART HOW A NATION CAME TOGETHER TO PREPARE FOR WAR

DAILY MIRROR, Saturday, April 1, 1939.

Daily Mirror

No. 11,020.   ONE PENNY.
Registered at the G.P.O. as a Newspaper.
Geraldine House, Fetter-lane, E.C.4.
HOLBORN 4321.

Symbol of the stand at last made against German aggression.

The flags of Britain and of France . . and with them the eagle of Poland on its ground of red and white.

HITLER FURIOUS AT BRITISH PLEDGE —U.S. PLEASED

PREMIER: ALL SUPPORT IN OUR POWER

THE Prime Minister's statement in the House of Commons yesterday was:

"As I said this morning, his Majesty's Government have no official confirmation of the rumours of any projected attack on Poland, and they must not therefore be taken as accepting them as true.

"I am glad to take this opportunity of stating again the general policy of his Majesty's Government. They have constantly advocated the adjustment by way of free negotiation between the parties concerned of any differences that may arise between them.

"In their opinion there should be no question incapable of solution by peaceful means, and they would see no justification for the substitution of force or threats of force for the method of negotiation.

Assurance to Poles

"As the House is aware, consultations are now proceeding with other Governments.

"In order to make perfectly clear the position of his Majesty's Government in the meantime, before those consultations are concluded, I now have to inform the House that during that period, in the event of any action which clearly threatened Polish independence and which the Polish Government accordingly considered it vital to resist with their national forces, his Majesty's Government would feel themselves bound at once to lend the Polish Government all support in their power.

"They have given the Polish Government an assurance to this effect.

"I may add that the French Government have authorised me to make it plain that they stand in the same position in this matter as do his Majesty's Government."

Soviet Consulted

In reply to Mr Arthur Greenwood (for the Labour Opposition), Mr. Chamberlain said that his statement was meant to cover an "interim period," that the Government was consulting other Powers, including the Soviet Union, and that the Soviet Ambassador and the Foreign Secretary had had a very full discussion.

"I have no doubt," added the Premier, "the principles on which we are acting are fully understood and appreciated by the Soviet."

When Colonel Beck, the Polish Foreign Minister, comes to London, added Mr. Chamberlain, there will be discussion of "further measures."

Mr. Greenwood pressed this question:—

"Could the Prime Minister say whether he would welcome that maximum co-operation from all the Powers, including U.S.S.R. ?"

"Yes, we should welcome the maximum amount of co-operation," said the Premier.

Debate, page 27. Hore-Belisha says "Join the Ranks," page 7.

FOR THE FIRST TIME SINCE 1914, BRITAIN TOLD THE WORLD YESTERDAY THAT SHE WAS READY TO FIGHT IN EUROPE TO STOP FURTHER GERMAN AGGRESSION.

Mr. Chamberlain, speaking with the knowledge and approval of America, France and Russia, said in the House of Commons:

"In the event of action which threatened Polish independence and which Poland considered it vital to resist, Britain would feel bound at once to lend the Polish Government all support in her power."

The Premier added: "The French Government have authorised me to make it plain that they stand in the same position as do His Majesty's Government."

That declaration had immediate reaction throughout the world.

It enraged Hitler, who tore up the speech he had prepared to make to-day at Wilhelmshaven.

There was great excitement in the Berlin Foreign Office and the Chancellery.

Hitler sent for his secretary, says Reuter, and re-dictated entirely those passages of his speech dealing with foreign affairs.

In Warsaw it is reported that military talks between the General Staffs of Britain, France and Poland have already begun.

Some British and French warships, says Associated Press, may be loaned to Poland.

What of Danzig?

And as the news spread through Warsaw that Poland would not fight alone, there was general rejoicing. It means "equal peace for east and west," was the official comment. One spokesman said:

"The matter is simple. If Germany does not respect our frontiers, we fight."

The special position of Danzig and the Polish Corridor as they are affected by the British pledge has not yet been made clear.

German newspapers last night reflected the anger of the Nazi leaders. A violent anti-British campaign was soon in full blast.

"It is absolutely incomprehensible how Mr. Chamberlain came to make such an announcement out of the blue," says a statement issued by the official German News Agency.

"One can only regard this statement by the British Premier as a laughable attempt to stir up unrest and sow mistrust of Germany in the concert of the nations.

"The whole thing gives the impression that Britain can only make the small Powers, if any, believe she is prepared to take action. In

(Continued on back page)

BOMB IN PARK LANE

EXPLOSION of a bomb blew out the window of a lingerie shop in Park-lane, W., early to-day.

Women in evening dress from the mannequin ball at the Dorchester, fifty yards away, ran into the street, believing that an entire building had blown up.

Extensive damage was done to the lingerie shop, which is next door to a bank, in a recently opened block of flats. But no one was injured.

About an hour before a bomb had shattered the windows of the "News-Chronicle" offices in Fleet-street.

Parts of the window were hurled by the force of the explosion right across the street, and there was a gaping hole in the masonry underneath the glass.

The explosion is believed to have been caused by a fuse bomb which was lit only a few minutes before.

TALKING OF SANDWICHES...

HAVE YOU TRIED FRY'S CHOCOLATE SANDWICH?

2d 2oz   4d. per ½ lb.

RED LABEL—Double Milk (plain chocolate between two layers of milk).
BLUE LABEL—Milk (milk chocolate between two layers of plain).

Left: Britain takes a stand against Hitler

Opposite: King George VI and Queen Elizabeth visit a barrage balloon station at RAF Hook

DAILY MIRROR, Wednesday, August 23, 1939.

Daily Mirror

No. 11,142   ONE PENNY

Registered at the G.P.O. as a Newspaper.
Geraldine House, Fetter-lane, E.C.4.
HOLBORN 4321.

BRITAIN ACTS— GOVT. RUSH BILL TO MEET CRISIS

BRITAIN'S course of action is decided.

Parliament meets to-morrow and will immediately pass an Emergency Powers (Defence) Bill, empowering the Government to take any necessary measures without delay.

Certain members of the Fighting and National Defence Services will be called up.

THESE DECISIONS WERE MADE DURING A CABINET MEETING LASTING FROM 3 P.M. TO 6.20 P.M. YESTERDAY, WHEN THE FOLLOWING STATEMENT WAS ISSUED:

" The Cabinet at their meeting to-day considered the international situation in all its bearings.

" In addition to a report that had been received as to military movements in Germany, the Cabinet took note of the report that a non-aggression pact between the German and Soviet Governments was about to be concluded.

" THEY HAD NO HESITATION IN DECIDING THAT SUCH AN EVENT WOULD IN NO WAY AFFECT THEIR OBLIGATIONS TO POLAND, WHICH THEY HAVE REPEATEDLY STATED IN PUBLIC, AND WHICH THEY ARE DETERMINED TO FULFIL.

" Parliament has been summoned to meet on Thursday next, when the Government propose to invite both Houses to pass through all its stages the Emergency Powers (Defence) Bill.

" The effect of this will be to place the Government in a position to take any necessary measures without delay should the situation require it.

" In the meantime, other measures of a precautionary character are being taken by the departments—for instance, the calling up of certain personnel for the Navy, Army and Royal Air Force, and for A.R.P. and civil defence.

" Arrangements are also being made to deal with certain matters affecting the export from this country of essential materials and commodities.

No Call For Force

" While taking these measures of precaution, which the Government consider necessary at this time, they remain of opinion that there is nothing in the difficulties that have arisen between Germany and Poland which would justify the use of force involving a European War, with all its tragic consequences.

" As the Prime Minister has repeatedly stated, there are indeed no questions in Europe which should not be capable of peaceful solution if only conditions of confidence could be restored.

" HIS MAJESTY'S GOVERNMENT ARE.

Continued on Back Page

Continued on Back Page

King's Return

The King, who is at Balmoral, was kept closely in touch with political events throughout yesterday.

Late last night, in well-informed Court circles, it was considered probable that the King would decide to-day to return to London.

In the 1938 September crisis the King, at the Premier's request, cancelled a visit to Glasgow, where he was to have launched the giant liner Queen Elizabeth, and remained in London.

The Queen went north alone and performed the ceremony.

+ + +

M.P.s were summoned to London from their holidays for to-morrow's meeting of Parliament in a message broadcast last night.

This was the first time in history that they had been recalled by radio.

They will meet at 2.45 p.m. to-morrow.

BRITISH NOTE TO HITLER ?

SIR NEVILE HENDERSON, the British Ambassador in Berlin, is expected to see Hitler at Berchtesgaden this morning, according to the Berlin correspondent of the Havas Agency.

It is reported, the correspondent says, that the British Ambassador will be the bearer of a message from Mr. Chamberlain.—Reuter.

Key to Soviet Move

The proposed non-aggression pact between the Soviet Union and Germany does not mean that a defensive alliance of Russia, Britain and France is impossible.

This statement, made last night in authoritative Soviet quarters, gives the key to the motives behind the Russian move that set the world guessing.

It revealed that Russia still wishes to bring the Anglo-Soviet talks to a successful conclusion.

Last night a conference between M. Molotoff, Soviet Premier and Foreign Commissar, Sir William Seeds, the British Ambassador, and M. Naggiar, the French Ambassador, was held in the Kremlin, Moscow.

And the Anglo-French-Soviet staff talks are going on.

Furthermore it is stated that the Pact contains a provision (which, in fact, exists in other Soviet non-aggression pacts), that it can be denounced if either side commits an act of aggression against a third country.

It is also stated that other clauses will be: An undertaking that neither side will attack the other; and an undertaking to remain neutral if the other is the victim of aggression.

A French view is that the Pact would simply be a matter of reaffirmation of treaties which already link Moscow and Berlin—the Treaty of Rapallo, of 1922, and the German-Soviet Neutrality Treaty of 1926. This second treaty could be considered a pact of non-aggression, and Hitler solemnly confirmed it in 1933.

The Japanese realise this and they were reported last night as being " on edge."

Although von Ribbentrop arrives in Moscow to-day, Tass, the Soviet official News Agency, said yesterday that the pact talks " may require some time." Thus, the agreement may not be signed so quickly as was at first thought.

Washington observers say Stalin, who is asking a high price for an agreement with Britain and France, is unlikely to be asking a lower price from Hitler, or allowing him a free hand in Eastern Europe.

A Warsaw statement said " There is no defeatism in Poland, and this country is fully prepared to fulfil its responsibility as regards the protection of peace and justice in Eastern Europe."

Messages: " Daily Mirror," Reuter, British United Press, Associated Press.

★ Hitler's 'Bitter Lesson' for Japan ★

Tokio observers say Japan has had a " bitter lesson in the spiritual bond " of the Anti-Comintern Pact and that there is no weight in Hitler's realistic policies. Newspaper comment is that a new situation faces Japan. The " Japan Times " says: " All things must be studied from new angles."

" All things " include Japan's present anti-British campaign.

Baron Hiranuma, Japanese Premier, and General Itagaki, War Minister, are to consider to-day how to adapt Japan's diplomacy to the new situation.

RAIL STRIKE

LOCOMOTIVE drivers and firemen are to go on strike at midnight on Saturday.

The Associated Society of Locomotive Engineers and Firemen reached that decision in London last night.

The railway companies expect the Government to intervene.

Full story on page 3.

DAILY MIRROR, Monday, August 28, 1939.

Daily Mirror

No. 11,146   ONE PENNY

Registered at the G.P.O. as a Newspaper.

.... there is our sure faith that, through endurance and courage, we can save the world from one of the most ruthless and desperate tyrannies that have ever threatened mankind.—See W.M. on page 11.

HITLER REFUSES TALK: DEMANDS DANZIG

WHILE THE BRITISH REPLY TO HITLER WAS BEING DRAFTED YESTERDAY THE GERMAN CHANCELLOR WAS FLATLY REFUSING TO ENTER NEGOTIATIONS WITH POLAND FOR A PEACEFUL SOLUTION TO THE CRISIS.

HITLER'S REFUSAL WAS CONTAINED IN A MESSAGE FLOWN TO M. DALADIER IN PARIS LAST NIGHT. IT WAS HANDED TO HIM BY A GERMAN ENVOY. THE INTERVIEW LASTED TWO MINUTES.

THEN AN OFFICIAL STATEMENT WAS ISSUED. IT ANNOUNCED THAT DALADIER HAD IMMEDIATELY ANSWERED HITLER'S STATEMENT TO THE AMBASSADORS LAST FRIDAY WITH A PROPOSAL THAT GERMANY AND POLAND SHOULD NEGOTIATE.

HITLER REFUSED. AND THE REFUSAL WAS CONFIRMED IN LAST NIGHT'S MESSAGE.

At 12.15 this morning a Press conference was hurriedly called in Berlin. The German journalists were handed copies of a long letter which Hitler has sent to Daladier.

Hitler declared that he has frequently shown his sympathy towards France.

But, the Fuehrer wrote, Danzig and the Corridor must return to the Reich.

"Corridor Must Return"

"I make a clear demand. Danzig and the Corridor must be returned.

"If fate should force us to fight again, I should be fighting to right a wrong.

"I am aware of the consequences, the heaviest of which would fall on Poland, because, however the fight ended, Poland would not exist as the same State."

France has been answered. The fate of Europe now rests on the German reply to the British message approved by the Cabinet yesterday.

That note will be flown back to Berlin to-day by Sir Nevile Henderson.

Hitler's answer is expected in London to-morrow, and Parliament will probably meet on Wednesday to consider the situation.

The British Note was drafted at a lengthy conference of Ministers, and the Cabinet meeting, which had been planned for 10.30 a.m., did not take place until 3 o'clock.

It lasted for an hour and three-quarters.

When it ended an official statement was issued announcing to-day's meeting of the Cabinet and Sir Nevile Henderson's journey to Berlin. The statement added:

"The reports which have appeared as to the contents of Herr Hitler's communication to the British Government are entirely unauthorised and quite inaccurate."

Premier Sees the King

The British Note, writes the Daily Mirror Diplomatic Correspondent, will be a firm refusal to withdraw from her obligations to Poland. It will answer every point raised by Hitler.

Whitehall continues to admire Poland's calm handling of the situation. The Poles are confident they can resist and their 'planes are in readiness to bomb Berlin.

When the Cabinet had dispersed amid the cheers of the waiting crowd, the Prime

Continued on Back Page

MYSTERY MAN AT EMBASSY

A MYSTERY man who arrived in England by air yesterday spent three hours at the German Embassy in Carlton House-terrace, London,—and is thought to have flown to Germany last night.

He arrived at the Embassy in a Diplomatic Corps car. All he would say when he left after three hours was: "I don't know who I am."

He said it rather sadly and shook his head. He spoke in good English, with the trace of a foreign accent. Then he was driven away.

An hour later three men arrived in a car at Heston Airport. One was seen off in a German 'plane understood to be bound for Amsterdam and Berlin. The airport officials would not say who he was.

The visitor to the Embassy was a tall, sunburned man, in a grey striped suit and black Homburg hat, carrying gloves and an umbrella.

He jumped out of the Diplomatic Corps car shortly before 3 p.m.

He did not appear to know by which door to enter the Embassy.

After his three hours' visit, he left by the car in which he had arrived.

Having refused to tell his name, he was pressed to say if he had arrived by air from Croydon or elsewhere. He waved his hand in a gesture that might have meant agreement or denial, and the car sped away.

He Watched Crowds

The car was driven into Belgravia by a roundabout route which included Pall Mall, The Mall, Horse Guards-parade (where there were crowds of sightseers), Birdcage-walk, and past Buckingham Palace, where there were also a number of spectators.

The car slowed down near the Horse Guards-parade, as if the passengers wished to look at the crowds by the Foreign Office and in Downing-street, but did not stop.

Information about the identity of the caller was not available at the Embassy.

Heston Airport officials received the three men who arrived at the port.

One man, who had a small travelling case, was taken to a German three-engine air liner, the Gustav Boelcke.

Five minutes later the 'plane set off.

Airport officials refused to answer any questions about the traveller.

The two men who had arrived with him were driven away immediately.

Duchess of Kent Flies Home

The Duchess of Kent returned to London yesterday by air from France. She flew in the King's private 'plane, piloted by Wing-Commander E. H. Fielden, Captain of the King's Flight.

The Duchess, who has been on holiday with the Duke of Kent, remained behind in Yugoslavia when the Duke returned to London earlier in the week.

Her sister is the wife of Prince Regent Paul of Yugoslavia.

Navy Controls All Ships

All British merchant ships are now under Admiralty control.

From midnight on Saturday every British ship afloat came under Admiralty direction.

Merchant ships must now obey any instructions given them, including any change of course found necessary by the Navy authorities.

15

16

We all stand together:
Crowds gathered through
day and night to watch
ministers and diplomats
arriving at Downing Street
after hearing that Nazi
Germany had invaded
Poland on September 1

18

19

Zero hour: Downing Street awash with people as Britain's 11am deadline of the ultimatum to Germany expired

Right: A news reel cameraman wearing a tin helmet films the crowds of people outside the Houses of Parliament as they react to the declaration of war

Below: Police keep crowds under control in Downing Street shortly after the Prime Minister's braoadcast to the nation declaring war on Germany

"STAND CALM, UNITED —WE SHALL PREVAIL": THE KING

UNITED, THE EMPIRE'S SYMBOL

Here is a historic picture. It was taken in Buckingham Palace last night immediately after the King had broadcast his message to his people in all parts of the Empire.

The King and Queen stood in their sitting-room, linked arm-in-arm, as so many thousands of their subjects may have been while the King spoke to them—Britons to Britons.

SEATED alone in his study in Buckingham Palace, the King broadcast to his people last evening. In serious, measured tone, he said:

" In this grave hour, perhaps the most fateful in our history, I send to every household of my people, both at home and overseas, this message, spoken with the same depth of feeling for each one of you as if I were able to cross your threshold and speak to you myself.

" For the second time in the lives of most of us we are at war. Over and over again we have tried to find a peaceful way out of the differences between ourselves and those who are now our enemies.

" But it has been in vain. We have been forced into a conflict. For we are called, with our allies, to meet the challenge of a principle which, if it were to prevail, would be fatal to any civilised order in the world.

" It is the principle which permits a State, in the selfish pursuit of power, to disregard its treaties and its solemn pledges; which sanctions the use of force, or threat of force, against the sovereignty, and independence of other States."

His voice rose a little, the pace of his words increased, as he declared:

" Such a principle, stripped of all disguise, is surely the mere primitive doctrine that might is right; and if this principle were established throughout the world, the freedom of our own country and of the whole British Commonwealth of Nations would be in danger.

Breaking Bondage of Fear

" But far more than this—the peoples of the world would be kept in the bondage of fear and all hopes of settled peace and of the security of justice and liberty among nations would be ended.

" This is the ultimate issue which confronts us. For the sake of all that we ourselves hold dear, and of the world's order and peace, it is unthinkable that we should refuse to meet the challenge.

" It is to this high purpose that I now call my people at home and my peoples across the seas, who will make our cause their own. I ask them to stand calm and firm and united in this time of trial.

" The task will be hard. There may be dark days ahead, and war can no longer be confined to the battlefield. But we can only do the right as we see the right, and reverently commit our cause to God.

" If one and all we keep resolutely faithful to it, ready for whatever service or sacrifice it may demand, then, with God's help, we shall prevail.

" May He bless and keep us all."

The King wore the dark blue undress uniform of an Admiral of the Fleet. As he spoke, the Queen listened in another room.

When Britain entered the war at eleven o'clock, the King and Queen were together in their private rooms at the Palace.

21

THEY PACKED UP THE
IN THEIR OLD KITBAGS & SMILE

With smiles mothers waved good-bye at school gates. They know their kiddies will be sa

ALONE in London

And with all the swings and sand-pit to play with!

They Thought This Was First Class

And by gum it was an' all! They travelled to their safety resort like lords and ladies. And you'll notice the holiday feeling showing in their faces.

Right: Her doll is evacuated with this little hospital patient when she left by Green Line coach for the country air.

THE ABO
ARRI

at a jolly looking house
Mothers, here's your count
like her.

Right: The start of th
fashion, with parcels, kitba
line up ready for the wor

TROUBLES
SMILED, SMILED

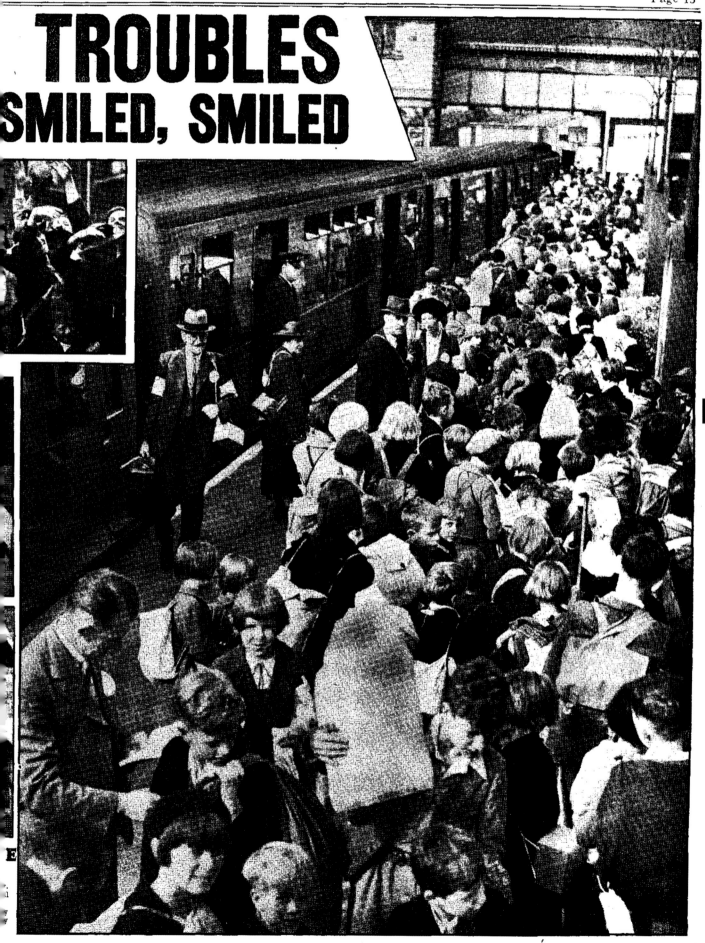

23

BRITISH FIGHTER No. 1

Up to now he's been behind the scenes, and all too few words have been written about him.

Viscount Gort, the V.C. who leads Britain's forces in the critical days ahead, is introduced in this intimate study.

You will know him better when you've finished this page.

ACROSS the dazzling snow of a Swiss slope two skiers move.

They gain speed.

Their speed is good; their sense of direction, rotten.

They collide.

Two shapes roll in a flurry of snow

They arise, puff, glare.

"Who the hell are you?" snorts one.

"Gort," snaps the other. "and who are you?"

"Hore-Belisha!"

And that was how Leslie Hore-Belisha, Britain's War Minister, first met Tiger Gort, who is to-day Britain's Number One soldier.

✦ ✦ ✦

That tumble in the snow finds an unexpected sequel in these stern days.

Co-operation between Hore-Belisha and Tiger Gort.

Co-operation between the Right Man in Whitehall and the Right Man on the field.

What manner of man is he who stands at the head of our Army?

His name: John Standish Surtees Prendergast Vereker, sixth Viscount Gort.

His decorations: V.C., C.B.E., D.S.O., M.V.O., M.C.

His age: Fifty-three—and a young fifty-three.

Titles and decorations cannot make a great soldier.

A surer guide is the nickname his men give him.

So mark well the Tiger that the men put before "Gort."

For he hasn't been nicknamed idly.

Twenty years have passed since the world last saw his extraordinary personal courage, his terrific strength, his unwavering spirit.

Yet twenty years have scarcely changed the man, physically.

He is still lean and hard. His eyes have not lost their keen, cold fire. His moustache is cropped even more closely

Indeed he looked very much as he does to-day on a certain September day in 1918.

You must picture him as he leads the crack 1st Battalion of the Grenadier Guards towards the Canal du Nord, near Flesquieres.

He leads his men into a storm of steel.

The "heavies" hurl eruptions of earth and mud to the sky. Machine-gun fire rakes the path of the advance

But the Guards reach their "forming-up" ground—only to meet a blast of fire more withering than any they have known.

Gort stumbles He has been hit

The man's strength comes to his aid. His voice sounds through the cannonade, directing a platoon down a sunken road to make a flanking attack.

The bombardment swells to a bursting wave of flame and sound that fills heaven and earth

✦ ✦ ✦

Over open ground Tiger Gort runs towards a British tank which is in difficulties. He leads the way, guiding the tank to a position where it can work most effectively.

But no man can expose himself so fearlessly and escape the fury of the bombardment.

A shell explodes near him. The flying shrapnel tears through flesh and sinew and bone.

Tiger Gort is down again.

A weaker man would have lapsed into unconsciousness.

Tiger Gort lies on a stretcher for a while.

Then, ignoring the protests of the ambulance men, he drags himself to his feet and returns to the thick of the fight.

Wounded and weakened by loss of blood, he personally directs the further attack.

His men, inspired by bravery which seems superhuman, fight like demons.

They capture more than 200 prisoners, two batteries of field guns and many machine-guns.

But the Tiger's work is not over yet.

He organises the defence of the captured position, attends to the hundred and one details, neglect of which may turn victory into defeat.

Then, man of iron though he has proved himself, Tiger Gort collapses.

Even then he does not leave the field Only when the "success signal" goes up on the final objective does he retire.

They gave him the V.C. for that day's work.

This high award was the climax of his war career; he had already won the D.S.O. three times and had been mentioned nine times in dispatches.

When peace came Tiger Gort was a Major-General. He had reached no higher rank than captain when war broke out.

Had it not been for the Great War, this fine soldier might have passed into an obscure retirement

Tiger Gort and Leslie Hore-Belisha had many talks. Neither knew what the future was to bring—but only six months later Hore-Belisha was War Minister and was looking around for a new Military Secretary.

He needed someone with energy and drive, someone mature enough to have ample experience but young enough to retain elastic ideas.

"Gort's the man," said Hore-Belisha.

"Impossible!" the veteran brass-hats snorted. "Why, he's only a major-general. Gad, sir, it's preposterous."

✦ ✦ ✦

But Hore-Belisha proved he had a way of dealing with the die-hards.

He drove down to Aldershot, sought out Tiger Gort, who was on manoeuvres—and appointed him Military Secretary.

If the brass-hats snorted at this, they nearly collapsed at the events of the next few months.

For the major-general became a lieutenant-general.

And then he was promoted Chief of the Imperial General Staff—slap over the heads of thirty generals!

Tiger Gort is not an easy master.

His passion for efficiency, his refusal to countenance excuses for mistakes, have made some of his subordinates wonder whether a man or a machine sits at that War Office desk.

Certainly his approach to reorganisation problems has all the ruthless efficiency of a machine.

He has slashed at the red tape which for generations impeded progress in many War Office departments.

He has become the most "air-minded" Army chief of our time.

He has established direct and regular contact with the commanders under him.

He has worked hard to improve the life of the private soldier.

So far a splendid machine.

✦ ✦ ✦

And perhaps the most revealing thing ever written about the man behind the uniform was penned by a woman. By a widow.

Her name was Mrs. Louisa Thiele, of St Leonards.

She lost her own child.

But in the little boy who was to become Viscount Gort she saw the ideal of the child she had lost

She watched him grow. She followed his progress at school; in the Army

And when she died she left this tribute to his character:

"I wish to express to him that the great happiness of my life has been in watching his fine character develop itself, his successful career, and the use of his talents, wealth and position in the unselfish service of his country."

Tiger Gort has heard many congratulatory addresses in his time.

But never a tribute that touched him more deeply.

OUR FAITH !

In the grim and grievous moments of this solemn day—A task is set before us—and within our hearts we pray—for guidance in the darkness of this great calamity—and power to bear the heavy burdens of our destiny.

The sword of justice is unsheathed by our reluctant hands—Deeply have we yearned for Peace. But now the hour demands—a strengthening in fibre of the soul and of the will. We have a pledge to honour and a purpose to fulfil.

This our task . . . To guard the things that freeborn men hold dear—and rid the world of brute aggression, tyranny and fear . . . To keep the way of life for which we've paid so high a price—the things that we have purchased with the blood of Sacrifice.

By Patience Strong

Popeye on a Haunted Ship!

DAILY MIRROR, Monday, September 4, 1939

Daily Mirror

No. 11,152 ✦ ONE PENNY
Registered at the G.P.O. as a Newspaper.

BRITAIN'S FIRST DAY OF WAR: CHURCHILL IS NEW NAVY CHIEF

POLES ATTACK

POLISH troops are fighting on German territory, according to a Warsaw message.

A Polish counter-attack pushed back the Germans and penetrated East Prussia near Deutsch Eylau, it was claimed.

The Polish Embassy in London described a Nazi report that troops had cut the Corridor as "entirely false."

Later (according to the Havas Agency) the Polish Radio announced that Poland had retaken the frontier station of Zbazyn.

The German News Agency claimed that Nazi troops, operating on the Southern front had taken the town of Radomsko.

Radomsko, north of the industrial region round Kattowitz, is about forty miles from the Polish frontier.

1,500 Raid Casualties

The Poles' latest estimate of casualties in German air raids was issued last night in Warsaw.

It is alleged that 1,500 people were killed or injured in German air bombardment of open towns and villages during Friday and Saturday. A considerable proportion of the victims were women and children.

[The German Government had secured from

Contd. on Bk. Page, Col. 1

BRITAIN AND GERMANY HAVE BEEN AT WAR SINCE ELEVEN O'CLOCK YESTERDAY MORNING. FRANCE AND GERMANY HAVE BEEN AT WAR SINCE YESTERDAY AT 5 P.M.

A British War Cabinet of nine members was set up last night. Mr. Winston Churchill, who was First Lord of the Admiralty when Britain last went to war, returns to that post.

Full list of the War Cabinet is:—

PRIME MINISTER: Mr. Neville Chamberlain.
CHANCELLOR OF THE EXCHEQUER: Sir John Simon.
FOREIGN SECRETARY: Viscount Halifax.
DEFENCE MINISTER: Lord Chatfield.
FIRST LORD: Mr. Winston Churchill.

SECRETARY FOR WAR: Mr. Leslie Hore-Belisha.
SECRETARY FOR AIR: Sir Kingsley Wood.
LORD PRIVY SEAL: Sir Samuel Hoare.
MINISTER WITHOUT PORTFOLIO: Lord Hankey.

There are other Ministerial changes. Mr. Eden becomes Dominions Secretary, Sir Thomas Inskip goes to the House of Lords as Lord Chancellor, Lord Stanhope, ex-First Lord, becomes Lord President of the Council, Sir John Anderson is the Home Secretary and Minister of Home Security—a new title.

None of these is in the Cabinet, which is restricted to the Big Nine. These are the men who will be responsible for carrying on the war.

But Mr. Eden is to have special access to the Cabinet.

The Liberal Party explained last night that although Sir Archibald Sinclair had been offered a ministerial post, the Party had decided at this moment not to enter the Government.

"BREMEN IS CAPTURED"

—French Report

The £4,000,000 German liner Bremen was reported to have been captured yesterday and taken to a British port.

A report from a high French source stated that the Bremen was captured at 4 p.m., but the area in which the liner was captured was not mentioned.

A French Government radio station broadcast the report which was picked up by the Mutual Broadcasting System of America.—Associated Press and British United Press.

Petrol Will Be Rationed

The first meeting of the new war Cabinet took place last night. Mr. Churchill was the first to leave and the crowd broke into a cheer as he walked out. Mr. Hore-Belisha was driven away by a woman chauffeur in uniform.

The Premier went from Downing-street to Buckingham Palace where he stayed with the King for three-quarters of an hour.

It was announced last night that as from September 16 all petrol will be rationed. In the meantime all car owners are asked not to use their cars more than is vitally necessary.

To-day all banks throughout Britain will be closed.

Australia yesterday declared war on Germany. "Where Britain stands, stand the people of the Empire and the British world," said Prime Minister Menzies in a broadcast message last night.

New Zealand has cabled her full support to Britain. There is a rush of recruits in Canada. At Toronto a queue of 2,000 men lined outside the Recruiting Office.

Japan has assured Britain of her neutrality in the present war.

Britain's last two-hour ultimatum to Germany was revealed to the people of Britain in a memorable broadcast from Downing-street by Mr. Chamberlain at 11.15 yesterday morning. By that time

cont'd in Col. 4, Back Page

The King to His People

"The task will be hard. There may be dark days ahead. . . . But we can only do the right as we see the right, and reverently commit our cause to God. If one and all we keep resolutely faithful to it, ready for whatever service or sacrifice it may demand, then, with God's help, we shall prevail."

These words were broadcast by the King last night. And to every household in the country a copy of his message, bearing his own signature facsimile, will be sent as a permanent record. The full speech is on page 3.

In the Army now: British soldiers wearing carnations in their caps prepare to leave for France following the declaration of war in September 1939

Below: Prime Minister Neville Chamberlain with his Parliamentary private secretary Alec Douglas-Home. Pictured beneath them is the 1939 War Cabinet. Back row, from left: Sir Kingsley Wood, Winston Churchill - First Lord of the Admiralty, Leslie Hore-Belisha, Lord Hankey. Front: Lord Halifax - Foreign Secretary, Sir John Simon, Neville Chamberlain - Prime Minister, Sir Samuel Hoare and Lord Chatfield

WANTED!

FOR MURDER . . . FOR KIDNAPPING . . .
FOR THEFT AND FOR ARSON

Can be recognised full face by habitual scowl. Rarely smiles. Talks rapidly, and when angered screams like a child.

ADOLF HITLER
ALIAS
Adolf Schicklegruber,
Adolf Hittler or Hidler

Last heard of in Berlin, September 3, 1939. Aged fifty, height 5ft. 8½in., dark hair, frequently brushes one lock over left forehead. Blue eyes. Sallow complexion, stout build, weighs about 11st. 3lb. Suffering from acute monomania, with periodic fits of melancholia. Frequently bursts into tears when crossed. Harsh, guttural voice, and has a habit of raising right hand to shoulder level. DANGEROUS !

Profile from a recent photograph. Black moustache. Jowl inclines to fatness. Wide nostrils. Deep-set, menacing eyes.

FOR MURDER Wanted for the murder of over a thousand of his fellow countrymen on the night of the Blood Bath, June 30, 1934. Wanted for the murder of countless political opponents in concentration camps.

He is indicted for the murder of Jews, Germans, Austrians, Czechs, Spaniards and Poles. He is now urgently wanted for homicide against citizens of the British Empire.

Hitler is a gunman who shoots to kill. He acts first and talks afterwards.

No appeals to sentiment can move him. This gangster, surrounded by armed hoodlums, is a natural killer. The reward for his apprehension, dead or alive, is the peace of mankind.

FOR KIDNAPPING Wanted for the kidnapping of Dr. Kurt Schuschnigg, late Chancellor of Austria. Wanted for the kidnapping of Pastor Niemoller, a heroic martyr who was not afraid to put God before Hitler. Wanted for the attempted kidnapping of Dr. Benes, late President of Czechoslovakia. The kidnapping tendencies of this established criminal are marked and violent. The symptoms before an attempt are threats, blackmail and ultimatums. He offers his victims the alternatives of complete surrender or timeless incarceration in the horrors of concentration camps.

FOR THEFT Wanted for the larceny of eighty millions of Czech gold in March, 1939. Wanted for the armed robbery of material resources of the Czech State. Wanted for the stealing of Memelland. Wanted for robbing mankind of peace, of humanity, and for the attempted assault on civilisation itself. This dangerous lunatic masks his raids by spurious appeals to honour, to patriotism and to duty. At the moment when his protestations of peace and friendship are at their most vehement, he is most likely to commit his smash and grab.

His tactics are known and easily recognised. But Europe has already been wrecked and plundered by the depredations of this armed thug who smashes in without scruple.

FOR ARSON Wanted as the incendiary who started the Reichstag fire on the night of February 27, 1933. This crime was the key point, and the starting signal for a series of outrages and brutalities that are unsurpassed in the records of criminal degenerates. As a direct and immediate result of this calculated act of arson, an innocent dupe, Van der Lubbe, was murdered in cold blood. But as an indirect outcome of this carefully-planned offence, Europe itself is ablaze. The fires that this man has kindled cannot be extinguished until he himself is apprehended—dead or alive !

THIS RECKLESS CRIMINAL IS WANTED—DEAD OR ALIVE!

All the above information has been obtained from official sources and has been collated by CASSANDRA.

HITLER: A PUBLIC'S ENEMY

ADOLF HITLER'S MEGALOMANIA MADE HIM PUBLIC ENEMY NUMBER ONE AS HIS AMBITIONS
FORCED BRITAIN INTO BATTLE. THE MIRROR'S POSTER ON THE OPPOSITE PAGE SUMMED UP
THE FEELINGS OF THE COUNTRY AS NEW RECRUITS SIGNED UP FOR THE WAR EFFORT

Above: Passers-by look at a
tailor's shop window plastered
with copies of the Mirror's
Hitler Wanted poster

Above: A driver sends out a clear
message on the boot of his car the
day after Britain had declared war

Above: New recruits gargling with mouth wash

Left: Volunteers line up outside a Royal Naval recruiting station at the outbreak of war

Above: New recruits wait in line to be vaccinated before being sent overseas

Left: Members of the public digging a trench for a communal air raid shelter in their back gardens in East London

Below: Crowds make their way to an underground shelter as the air raid siren sounds

All For One & One For All

AS THE REALITY OF WAR HIT HOME, BRITAIN PREPARED FOR THE TROUBLES AHEAD.
FROM BUILDING AIR RAID SHELTERS AND SANDBAGGING TO TRIALING GAS MASKS
AND EVACUATION PROCEDURES, THE PEOPLE'S SPIRIT STARTED TO SHINE THROUGH

Warning sound: Crowds leave Downing Street after an air raid warning. They had gathered to hear Prime Minister Neville Chamberlain announce Germany's failure to withdraw from Poland had led to Britain declaring war on Germany

Left: Members of the Air Raid Precautions Services receive instruction before going out on an exercise

Above: Work continues on an A.R.P. air raid shelter in Durham

Right: Residents of Links Avenue, Monkseaton, show some community spirit by constructing their own communal air raid shelter

Above: Residents of Eltham, London try out an air raid shelter

Devastation: A cinema suffered severe damage during an enemy air raid over a North East coastal town

38

Masked men: Two air raid wardens cause a stir as they take a stroll in full regalia

Suffer the children: Youngsters at the Sunshine Home for blind babies at East Grimstead, Sussex, carry out a respiratory drill. They think it is a game and are not told the real reason for the gas masks

Below: Children are fitted with gas masks following distribution in the autumn of 1939

41

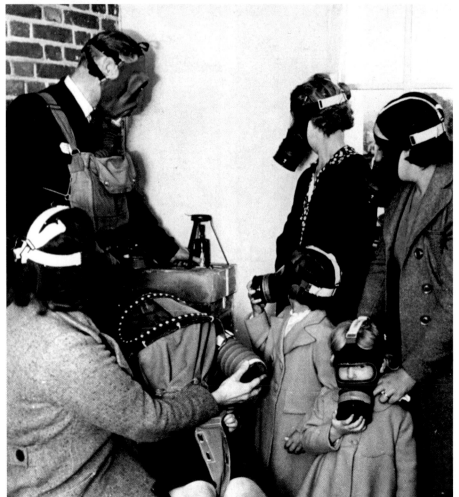

Above: Volunteer ambulance drivers wearing gas masks as they practise attending to a 'victim' as part of their training. The dustcart is used in place of an ambulance

Left: Officials at a new gas chamber for testing gas masks on the roof of the Guildhall in Kingston-upon-Thames. They are there to help reassure people that their masks are fitted correctly and work properly

Opposite: A baby in a gas mask smiles at her mother in August 1939

Above: Sewing sandbags in the East End of London

Right: Filling sandbags in Birmingham city centre

44

Left: Sandbags being piled up around the Town Hall in Birmingham at the outbreak of war

Below: Three policemen wearing tin helmets stand outside the sandbagged entrance to their police station in mid-September 1939

Left: Parents and children help sandbag the main entrance to Manchester Grammar School before it was reopened in October 1939

Watcher of the skies: An aircraft observer lies back in a chair on top of a sandbag enforcement scanning the skies for enemy aircraft

THE GRIM REALITIES OF WAR

THE PUBLICATION OF CASUALTY LISTS, CHANGES TO CONSCRIPTION RULES AND THE QUEEN'S CALL FOR WOMEN TO SHOW FORTITUDE ALL EMPHASISED THE HARSH REALITIES OF THE CONFLICT. CHILDREN WERE ALSO AFFECTED AS DEPICTED IN THE PAGES THAT FOLLOW

Tea for two: Children in full military uniform, reflecting the world they were born into

HER GUESTS BLESS THE QUEEN

FIVE mothers from working-class districts of Glasgow, their children soundly asleep in comfortable beds, sat round a wireless set in a mansion on the royal estate at Balmoral and listened intently to the Queen's Armistice Day message to women of the Empire.

"God bless her," they whispered, as the Queen said: "The King and I appreciate the hospitality shown by those of you who have opened your homes to strangers and to children sent from places of special danger."

There were tears of gratitude in the eyes of the women as they stood up at the end of the speech to sing the National Anthem.

For these evacuated mothers and their children are the guests of the Queen. Through her characteristic kindliness they have found peace and security in these days of war. Three weeks ago the families were billeted in quarters on the estate. By the express wish of the Queen, they were moved to Craigowan House, the mansion formerly occupied by Lord Wigram. Craigowan House is close to Balmoral Castle.

"Winter is coming on and I want them to have every comfort," said the Queen.

Each mother has been given a big room for herself and children, for whom a playroom has been opened. The mothers share the mansion's well-equipped kitchen to do their cooking.

In her broadcast, made as she sat alone in a room at Buckingham Palace the Queen paid tribute to the war work of the women of the Empire.

"We women, no less than the men, have real and vital work to do.

"The tasks you have undertaken, whether at home or in distant lands, cover every field of national service."

"At the same time, I do not forget the humbler part which so many of you have to play in these trying times. . . It is the thousand and one worries and irritations in carry-

"War has at all times called for the fortitude of women"—The Queen during her broadcast.

MORE MEN

THE twenty—twenty-one years Army Class is now liable to be called to the colours. A Royal Proclamation to this effect was issued last night.

The men will register at labour exchanges on a date to be announced, but calling-up notices may wait until November.

Provisional date for registration is October 21. Details are on page 2.

Men who reached the age of twenty-two yesterday will not register.

INNOCENT, BUT HITLER HAS STRUCK AGAIN

Full Story on Back Page

Amazing Picture

Pages 10 and 11

GERMANY SINKS —BRITAIN BANS

Britain is to fight the new Nazi frightfulness at sea by imposing fresh restrictions on German trade.

In future we shall seize all German exports carried in neutral ships.

This reprisal for the new and dastardly sea mine warfare will cut off the flow of neutral gold into Germany. But it will also seriously damage the trade of neutral States. They may well regard it as a hostile act.

Holland, one of the neutrals most affected, expressed its alarm last night after Mr. Chamberlain had announced the decision in the House of Commons.

One Dutch newspaper, voicing the general fear, said:

"Even before the final death roll in the Simon Bolivar disaster is known, some quarters are already preparing to forge a new weapon out of this disaster—a weapon which not only strikes at the enemy, but also against neutrals.

"Holland cannot understand why this disaster, of which Holland is the victim, should be utilised further to damage the interests of neutrals."

In Washington, Mr. Sumner Welles, Under-Secretary of State, said the United States had advised Britain that U.S.A. was not endorsing any principle of interference with its neutral trade.

Last to leave the ship . . . the Terukuni Maru's captain photographed as he stepped ashore after seeing that his 206 passengers and crew were safe.

Right: A motor launch towing boats to the sinking liner.

War baby: A soldier says goodbye to his daughter before leaving to serve his country

51

Above: Newcastle schoolchildren arrive at the Archbold Hall, Wooler, for their first meal after being evacuated from the city

Left: The headmaster of St Michaels Church School in Buckingham Palace Road instructs children for their evacuation the next day

Gimme shelters:
Excited children watch
the delivery of the first
consignment of A.R.P.
air raid shelters in the
Two Ball Lonnen area
of Newcastle

Helping hand:
Four-year-old
Andrew Paviour
in full uniform

Learning zone: Home schooling in Birmingham during October 1939

No place like home: Evacuated children from the cities play with toys in their new surroundings in September 1939

Right: Children of Pimlico, London packing for evacuation

Below: Bewildered-looking youngsters prepare to be evacuated from their Tyneside homes

54

Left: Schoolchildren evacuated from London during air raids

Below: War evacuees board a train at Euston Station

WOMEN AT WAR

WHILE HUSBANDS, FATHERS, BROTHERS AND BOYFRIENDS LEFT FOR COMBAT ON FOREIGN FIELDS, BRITAIN'S WOMEN PLAYED THEIR FULL PART IN THE WAR CAMPAIGN. THE PHOTOS THAT FOLLOW SHOW THE VARIOUS WAYS IN WHICH THEY CAME TO THEIR COUNTRY'S AID

Above: Auxiliary nurses marching in Esher

Right: The first million Players' cigarettes from the unity pool for the B.E.F. are dispatched in time to reach troops for Christmas

Left: Women from the Ministry of Supply vet applications for petrol coupons following the outbreak of war

Below: Fisherwomen viewing the catch at North Shields fish quay

We'll drink to that: ATS cooks
celebrate after lunch with a drink

58

Taste test: ATS cooks
preparing lunch

How's that? ATS cooks
show off their efforts

Left and below: Fulfilling duties
with the River Emergency Service

Above: Organisers at Newcastle's Women's Voluntary Services help to enrol new members

Right: A lady fits blackout shields to the headlamps of her car

Dual role: Elsie Creasy, a nurse at Jackney Hospital, doubled up as a member of the Civil Air Guard

Wedding Belle: The conflict didn't stop ATS Private Betty Coustable getting married in September 1939

High fashion: Away from the uniform of war, a lady models the latest look

Making news: A member of the Women's Auxiliary Air Force reviews the morning's news at the breakfast table

WAR OVER AIR, LAND AND SEA

WITH TROOPS FULLY MOBILISED, THE BATTLES BEGAN. THE IMAGES IN THIS SECTION PORTRAY THE HORRIFYING IMPACT OF WAR. PICTURED BELOW, CROWDS GATHER AT PLYMOUTH AS THE HMS EXETER RETURNS AFTER THE ALLIED VICTORY AT THE BATTLE OF THE RIVER PLATE

Up in smoke: A giant tanker,
Regent Tiger, explodes after being
torpedoed in the English Channel

Battle lines: The ships of the world laden with grain make their way into the sunset during the early stages of the Battle of the Atlantic. It lasted almost six years and was the longest continuous military campaign of the war

67

Setting sail: The British fleet at Invergordon, Scotland consisting of battleships HMS Rodney, HMS Resolution, HMS Royal Oak, HMS Royal Sovereign and battlecruiser HMS Repulse

Below: British soldiers have a hot tub in France

Bottom: RAF pilots and crews make their way to their Avro Anson planes in September 1939

At the ready: An anti-aircraft gun on the East Coast of Scotland

Paying their respects: Soldiers
visit a war cemetery in France

70

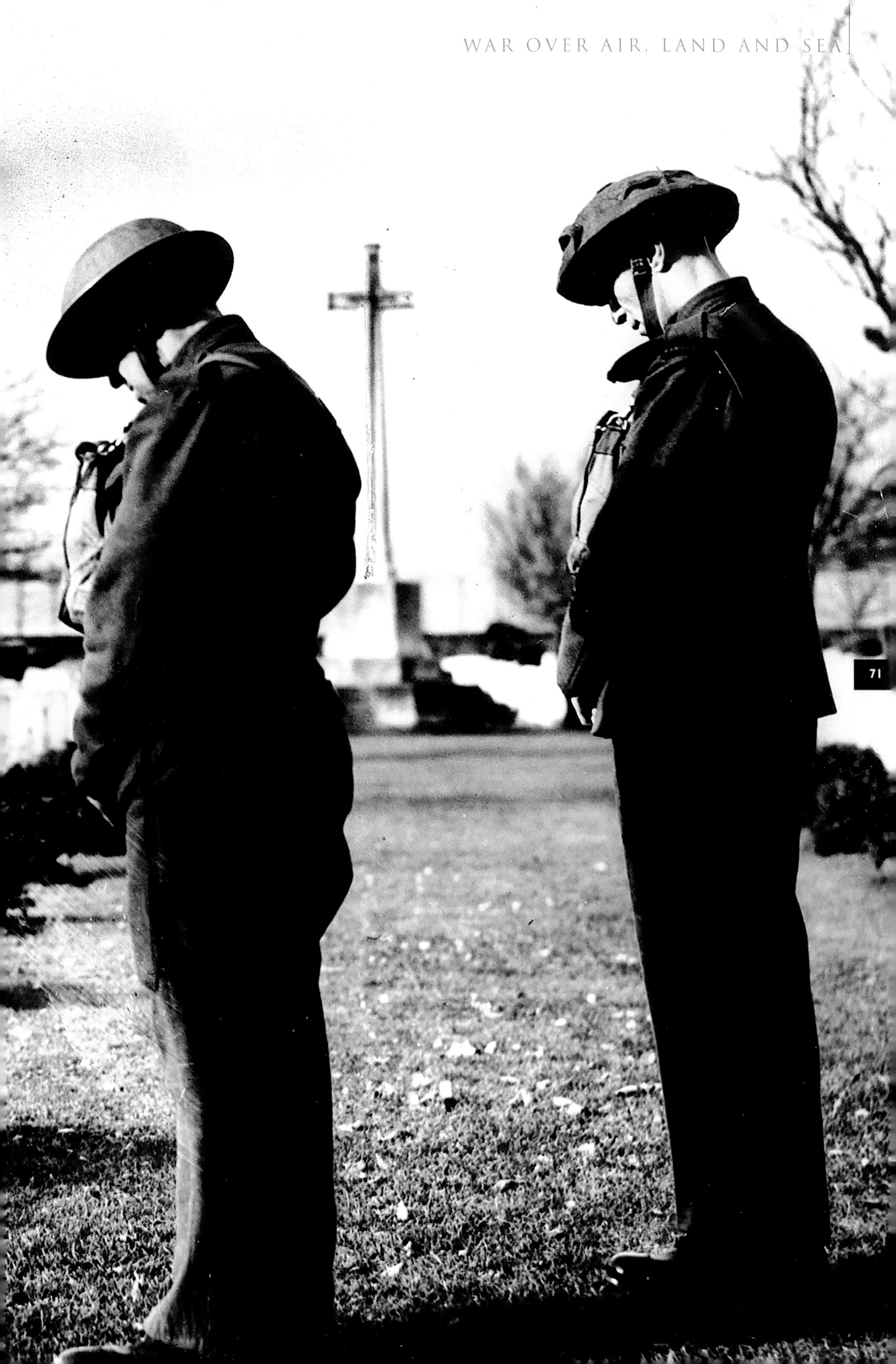

Above: Lieutenant General Sir John Dill inspecting soldiers at work digging trenches in France

Right: Jewish refugees on board the Polish liner Pilsudster at Newcastle Quay

HMS Royal Oak: The battleship was sunk by German U-boats at the Battle of Scapa Flow

Below: Inspectors check the quality of shells for naval guns in a munitions factory

Grounded: A Heinkel He 111 is brought down in Scotland

Above: An animal guard wearing the national ARP Animals helmet

Above: Concerned women cluster around a man rescued from the British Royal Navy aircraft carrier HMS Courageous which was sunk by German U-boat U-29

Below: A solemn service of prayer during High Mass at Westminster Cathedral following the outbreak of war

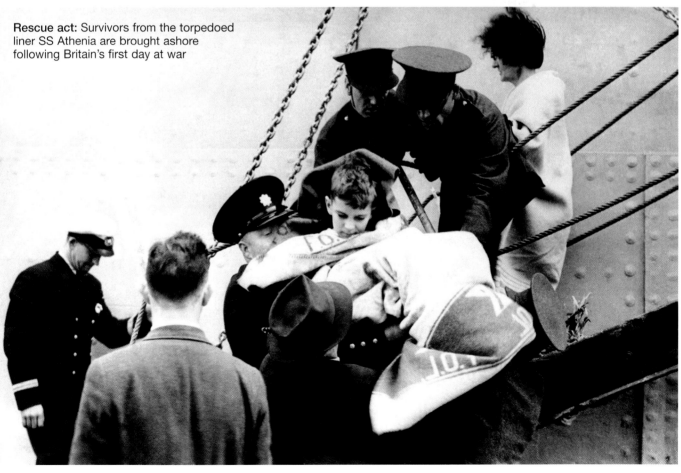

Rescue act: Survivors from the torpedoed liner SS Athenia are brought ashore following Britain's first day at war

HITLER'S ANS

"ictim of a

BRITAIN DECLARED WAR ON HITLER, BUT HITLER IS NOW DOING ALL THE FIGHTING.

His answer to us is sharp and challenging.

The triumphs of war are nobody's—yet.

But . . .

How are we going to retaliate? In war force must be met by force.

How much longer are we to tolerate the brutal sinking of the world's shipping?

The British Government last night were planning to meet Hitler's ruthless and triumphant force with—another trade ban. A feather matched against a sword.

For how long?

Still wearing their life-jackets, officers and crew of the Terukuni Maru on board a tender after being picked up. Plenty of smiles in both pictures. They've lost their ship, but . . .

All those boat drills have not been in vain, for when the emergency came everything went like clockwork, and their passengers were got safely away.

★

You owe the amazing pictures in today's "Daily Mirror" of the sinking of the Terukuni Maru to a boy of eighteen.

Horrified yet thrilled at the great sea drama taking place before him, he had the initiative to seize a camera and to record this latest Nazi outrage in pictures.

And he knew the right place to send his pictures . . . the offices of the "Daily Mirror."

His photographs will be well paid for. It won't be only camera work that will have earned him the money, but initiative and enterprise.

Japan's crack liner Teruku and sinking as boatloads of su

R TO OUR WAR

k Japanese liner, Terukuni Maru.

onal flag painted on her side, heeling over afety. Around her is other merchant ship- | ping, showing that the mine was deliberately laid in the path of neutral and British merchantmen . . . evidence of the ruthless barbarity of the Nazi mining campaign.

KEEP SMILING THROUGH

WITH THE DEATH TOLL RISING EACH DAY, THE FORCES AND THEIR FAMILIES WELCOMED A LITTLE LIGHT RELIEF WHENEVER OPPORTUNITY AROSE. BE IT A TRIP TO THE THEATRE OR A MIRROR CARTOON TO RAISE A SMILE, HERE'S HOW SOLACE WAS SOUGHT IN ENTERTAINMENT

Above: Soldiers attending a football match in 1939

Left: Comedian Sandy Powell and the cast of Can You See me Mother entertaining soldiers during the interval of a matinee performance at London Coliseum

Right: In Sussex, ENSA entertain troops awaiting their postings to the frontline

A SELECTION OF CARTOONS FROM THE DAILY MIRROR DURING THE EARLY DAYS OF THE WAR...

SUCTION!

STATIC
WATER

HOOK
LADDERS!

MAKING
UP!

SUNDAY PICTORIAL

ONWARD!

?

LEAGUE OF NATIONS
PALACE OF PEACE

HIT HIM
(NASTY JOE)
NOT
ME!
(PEACEFUL ADOLF)

TELL THAT TO THE MARINES, ADOLF!

Strength—Through Joy!

81